I0776738

The Story of a Special Day
Volume 198

July 16

The 197th day of the year (198th in leap years). There are 168 days remaining until the end of the year.

by Michael Dobson

Timespinner
Press

This book is also available in e-book form for Kindle, e-pub devices, and other formats from your favorite online booksellers.

For more information about the series, about us, or about your special day, please email us at editor@timespinnerpress.com.

Look for other volumes in *The Story of a Special Day,* coming often. See www.timespinnerpress.com for details and for the most recent information.

Table of Contents

Cover: The Apollo 11 mission takes off for the Moon, July 16, 1969 — the COVER STORY and EVENT OF THE DAY. (Credit: NASA)

Quote of the Day

"We knew the world would not be the same. A few people laughed, a few people cried, most people were silent. I remembered the line from the Hindu scripture, the *Bhagavad-Gita*; Vishnu is trying to persuade the Prince that he should do his duty and, to impress him, takes on his multi-armed form and says, 'Now I am become Death, the destroyer of worlds.' I suppose we all thought that, one way or another."

Robert Oppenheimer, scientific director of the Manhattan Project, about the first detonation of a nuclear weapon, which took place July 16, 1945

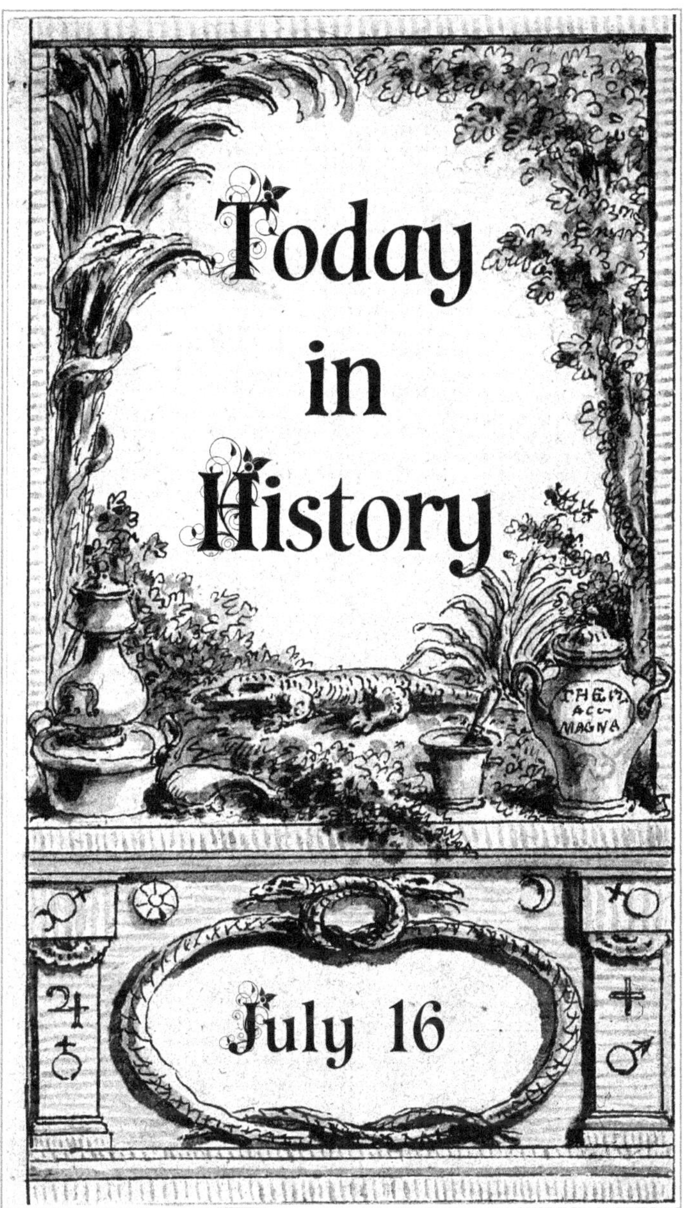

Today
in
History
July 16

July, by Eugène Grasset

July 16 in History

While some days of the year are more famous than others, every day of the year is filled with important, exciting, and unusual events, from religious awakenings to natural disasters, from wars to breakthroughs in technology, and from tragedy to triumph.

In this section, you'll learn about all the events that make July 16 important, including the special event that makes up our cover story or event of the day. Some events you may already know about, others may be new to you, but all of them are important parts of the history of the work. Illustrated events are shaded.

Let's explore some of the reasons why July 16 is a very special day!

Michael Dobson

Launch of Apollo 11

What Happened on July 16?

Apollo 11, the first manned mission to the Moon, took off from Kennedy Space Center's Launch Pad 39A on July 16, 1969. It would land on the Moon four days later, and return to Earth safely on July 24.

The Space Race between the Soviet Union and the United States effectively began with Soviet's launch of the launch of the first artificial satellite, Sputnik 1, on October 4, 1957. The US was less successful; the first Vanguard launch exploded on national television on December 6, 1957. It was not until January 1, 1958, that the US managed a successful satellite launch.

In 1959, President Dwight Eisenhower signed legislation to create the National Aeronautics and Space Administration (NASA), charged with the US space program. This transferred space efforts from the US Air Force to a new civilian agency, where the manned space flight efforts were given a new name: Project Mercury.

The Soviets continued to surge ahead. On April 12, 1961, cosmonaut Yuri Gagarin became the first human in space, completing a single orbit on April 12, 1961. Less than a month later, Alan Shepard became the first American in space, completing a suborbital flight.

These Soviet successes convinced US President John F. Kennedy of the necessity for strong leadership in the space effort, leading to his famous "We Choose to Go to the Moon" speech given in Houston on September 12, 1962.

With increased funding and support, the US launched five more missions in the Mercury program, including John Glenn's 1962 flight that completed three orbits of the Earth. The Soviets countered by launching two ships simultaneously, and on June 16, 1963, sent the first woman (and first civilian) into space, Valentina Tereshkova.

In the Gemini program, the US explored the technologies necessary to make the Moon flight, including space walks, space rendezvous, and docking. The Soviet Voskhod program pioneered three-astronaut crews and a "shirt sleeve" cabin environment, but political troubles in the Soviet Union put a long pause in their program and allowed the US to achieve parity. Ten Gemini missions gave the US a strong base of knowledge.

Both sides suffered setbacks. The first Apollo mission was destroyed when a cabin fire killed astronauts Gus Grissom, Ed White, and Roger Chaffee on the launch pad. Vladimir Komarov became the first in-flight fatality when his Soyuz 1 parachute failed on reentry.

Apollo 7 was the first Apollo mission to reach orbit, and 15 days later, the Soviets launched Soyuz 3, which attempted the first space docking. The race remained close, with both nations completing circumlunar flights in early 1969.

With both nations poised to go to the Moon, the race was increasingly tight. The Soviet N-1 rockets, however, suffered several launch failures and a major launch pad explosion. Meanwhile the US set a goal of a July 1969 lunar landing, to be achieved by Apollo 11.

The Apollo 11 crew was selected in January 1969. The Mission Commander was Neil Armstrong, the Command Module Pilot was Michael Collins, and the Lunar Module Pilot was Edwin "Buzz" Aldrin. Armstrong and Aldrin would go down to the surface of the Moon, while Collins would remain in the Command Module.

Crew of Apollo 11: From left, Neil Armstrong, Michael Collins, and Buzz Aldrin

Because the Apollo 10 crew named their spacecraft *Charlie Brown* and their lunar module *Snoopy*, the Apollo 11 crew was asked to be more serious in selecting names. They named the command module *Columbia* after Jules Verne's spacecraft in his 1865 novel *From the Earth to the Moon.* The lunar module was named *Eagle,* for the US national bird.

Millions watched the launch of Apollo 11 at 13:32:00 UTC* on July 16, 1969. It reached orbit twelve minutes after takeoff, and thirty minutes later fired its rockets again to head for the Moon. Once there, the spacecraft entered lunar orbit.

The *Eagle* in flight

---

* UTC: Coordinated Universal Time, an improved version of what was once known as "Greenwich Mean Time."

On Sunday, July 20, Armstrong and Aldrin entered the lunar module and began the descent to the Sea of Tranquility on the lunar surface. The mission nearly ended in failure when the onboard navigation and guidance computer overloaded, but the software recovered and the mission continued. Armstrong took manual control as the spacecraft neared the surface of the Moon, and at 20:17:40 UTC on July 20, they touched down on the lunar surface with only 25 seconds of fuel remaining. "Houston, Tranquility Base here," Armstrong transmitted. "The *Eagle* has landed."

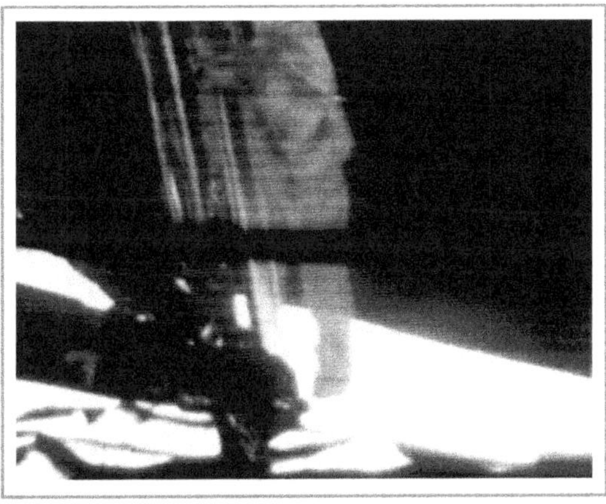

"One small step"

It took several hours to get ready to set foot on the Moon, but on 02:39 UTC on Monday, July 21, 1969, Neil Armstrong opened the hatch and climbed down the ladder, with each step transmitted back to Earth with a television signal watched by million. Armstrong meant to say "That's one small step for a man, one giant leap for mankind," as he set foot on the Moon, but the "a" got lost in transmission.

The astronauts planted an American flag and uncovered a plaque on the base of the ladder: "Here men from the planet Earth first set foot upon the Moon, July 1969 A.D. We came in peace for all mankind."

The astronauts stayed on the surface for around two and a half hours, then reentered the *Eagle*. They rested for about seven hours before preparing to leave the lunar surface and rejoin *Columbia*.

Just before dawn on July 24, the *Columbia* splashed down in the Pacific Ocean and the astronauts were recovered. Although the chance of bringing back a deadly disease from the Moon was considered remote, the astronauts were quarantined for 21 days just in case.

Today, the *Columbia* can be seen at the Smithsonian's National Air and Space Museum in Washington, DC.[†]

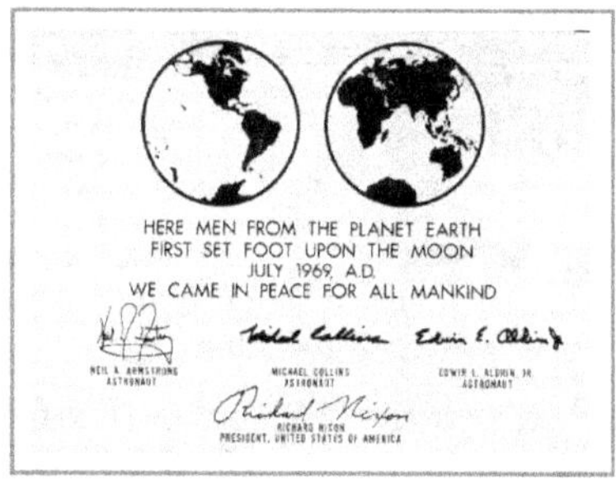

[†] Apollo 11 command module pilot Mike Collins became director of the National Air and Space Museum during the creation of the building on the National Mall; this author was privileged to be a member of the research staff during that time.

Astronaut Buzz Aldrin

A 17th century banknote issued by Stockholms Banco

The Mission San Diego de Alcalá in 1848

More July 16 Events

622 — The **Islamic calendar begins.** The first day of the first month of the Islamic calendar (1 Muharram 1 AH) corresponds to July 16, 622, on the Julian calendar, as determined by Muslim astronomers.

1661 — The **first European paper money** is issued by Stockholms Banco in Sweden. It is unsuccessful.

1769 — The Mission San Diego de Alcalá, which will later grow into the city of **San Diego**, California, is established.

1790 — The **District of Columbia**, the future site of Washington, DC, is established by law.

1861 — The first major land battle of the American Civil War, the **First Battle of Bull Run**, takes place, ending in a Confederate victory. *(Photo page 14.)*

1862 — **David Farragut** becomes the first officer in the US Navy to be promoted to admiral rank.

1915 — The **Order of the Arrow,** national honor society of the Boy Scouts of America, is founded.

1935 — The **world's first parking meter** is installed in Oklahoma City, Oklahoma.

1945 — The **Atomic Age begins** with the Trinity test, a detonation of the first nuclear weapon.

1948 — The **first aircraft hijacking** of a commercial plane takes place when a Cathay Pacific seaplane is taken over. All but the lead hijacker are killed; he is not prosecuted because of jurisdictional issues.

First Battle of Bull Run, by Kurz & Allison (1889)

The Trinity nuclear test at Alamogordo, New Mexico, July 16, 1945.
Mushroom cloud after ten seconds

Quote of the Day

"Victory awaits him who has everything in order — luck, people call it. Defeat is certain for him who has neglected to take the necessary precautions in time; this is called bad luck."

Roald Amundsen, Polar explorer
born July 16, 1872

Births
and
Deaths
CHEM
AC
MAGNA
July 16

Shoeless Joe Jackson (Photo: Charles M. Conlon). Baseball outfielder alleged to have participated in the Black Sox scandal conspiracy to fix the 1919 World Series, born July 16, 1887

Notable July 16 People

With the current world population at about seven billion people, on average about 19 million people also celebrate their birthdays on July 16 — and that isn't counting the millions and millions who came before! No matter when you were born, you share your birthday with many special people whose accomplishments (and occasionally embarrassments) have been noted as part of history.

In this section, you'll meet fascinating people who share your birthday. They're organized by what they're famous for, and then in reverse chronological order from most recent to earliest. Those who are shown in photographs or artwork have a box around them. We don't have photos of everyone, so please forgive us if your favorite person is missing.

Some of these people you've heard of, others may be new to you, but they all make up an important part of the reason that July 16 is a truly special day!

Ginger Rogers, actress and dancer, born July 16, 1911

Who Was Born on July 16?

Business

Orville Redenbacher, businessman and entrepreneur best known as the co-founder and public face of Orville Redenbacher brand popcorn. *(1907)*

Orville Redenbacher

Civil Rights and Women's Suffrage

Ida B. Wells, African-American journalist and editor; author of *Southern Horrors: Lynch Law in All Its Phases* and *The Red Record*; a founder of the National Association for the Advancement of Colored People (NAACP); also active in the women's rights and women's suffrage movement. *(1862)*

Ida B. Wells (Photo: Mary Garrity)

Exploration and Adventure

Roald Amundsen, Norwegian polar explorer, first to reach the South Pole, first to reach both poles, and first to navigate the Northwest Passage. *(1872)*

Roald Amundsen (Photo: Daniel Georg Nyblin)

Government and Politics

Trygve Lie, Norwegian politician who became the first Secretary-General of the United Nations. *(1896)*

Music and Dance

Michael Flatley, dancer and choreographer known for his Irish dance shows, including *Riverdance* and *Lord of the Dance. (1958)*

Michael Flatley (Photo: Max Lin, CC BY-SA 2.0)

Stewart Copeland, composer and musician best known as drummer for The Police; member of the Rock and Roll Hall of Fame. *(1952)*

Rubén Blades, Panamanian singer-songwriter and actor who won eight Grammy Awards and five Latin Grammy Awards; appeared in numerous television shows and films including *Fear the Walking Dead, The Milagro Beanfield War*, and *The Josephine Baker Story*. *(1948)*

Desmond Dekker, ska, rocksteady and reggae musician who had one of the earliest international reggae hits with 1968's "Israelites." *(1941)*

Denise LaSalle, singer-songwriter whose hits include "Trapped By a Thing Called Love;" member of the Blues Hall of Fame and the Rhythm and Blues Hall of Fame. *(1939)*

William Bell, soul singer best known for "You Don't Miss Your Water," "Tryin' to Love Two," and as the writer of the blues classic "Born Under a Bad Sign." *(1939)*

Tony Jackson, bass guitar player and singer best known as a member of The Searchers; hits include "Sweets for My Sweet," "Don't Throw Your Love Away," and "Love Potion No. 9." *(1938)*

Buddy Merrill, guitar player best known as a regular on The Lawrence Welk Show for nearly 20 years. *(1936)*

Performing Arts

AnnaLynne McCord, played Eden on the TV series *Nip/Tuck* and Naomi on *90210*. *(1987)*

Corey Feldman, actor whose best known films include *Gremlins, The Goonies, Stand by Me,* and *The Lost Boys*. *(1971)*

Will Ferrell, comedian, actor, and writer who came to fame as a cast member of Saturday Night Live; films include *Anchorman, Talledega Nights*, and *Elf*. *(1967)*

Sherri Stoner, voice actress and writer; producer of the animated series *Tiny Toon Adventures* and *Animaniacs*; created and voiced the character Slappy Squirrel. *(1965)*

Phoebe Cates, actress best known for roles in *Fast Times at Ridgemont High* and *Gremlins*. *(1963)*

Faye Grant, actress known as Juliet Parrish in the science fiction series *V* and its sequels. *(1957)*

Angharad Rees, actress best known as Demelza in the 1970s BBC drama *Poldark*. *(1944)*

Bess Myerson, Miss America 1945, first (and to date only) Jewish woman to win the title; served in several Presidential commissions and ran unsuccessfully for US Senate; panelist on *I've Got a Secret* and other game shows. *(1924)*

Bess Myerson

Ginger Rogers, actress, dancer, and singer best known for her ten films with Fred Astaire; won the Academy Award for Best Actress for *Kitty Foyle*. *(1911)* *(Photo page 20.)*

Barbara Stanwyck, actress who appeared in 85 Hollywood films; nominated for four Academy Awards for Best Actress, for *Stella Dallas, Ball of Fire, Double Indemnity,* and *Sorry, Wrong Number*. *(1907)*

Frances Horwich, best known as "Miss Frances," home of the long-running children's television program *Ding Dong School,* which at one time had a 95% viewing share among all preschoolers. *(1907)*

Mary Philbin, silent film actress best known for playing Christine opposite Lon Chaney in the 1925 film *The Phantom of the Opera*. *(1902)*

Larry Semon, actor and filmmaker during the silent film era, best known for directing and playing the Scarecrow in the 1925 silent film production of *The Wizard of Oz*. *(1889)* *(Photo page 30.)*

Percy Kilbride, actor best known for playing Pa Kettle in the *Ma and Pa Kettle* film series. *(1888)* *(Photo page 30.)*

Religion

Mary Baker Eddy, founder of the Christian Science movement; author of *Science and Health with Key to the Scriptures*. *(1821)*

Barbara Stanwyck in *Stella Dallas* (1937)

Larry Semon

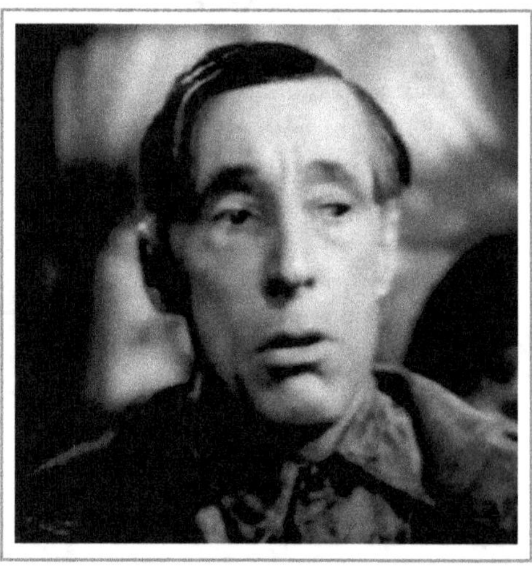

Percy Kilbride, in *George Washington Slept Here* (1942)

Science

Irwin Rose, biologist who shared the 2004 Nobel Prize in Chemistry for the discovery of ubiquitin-mediated protein degradation. *(1926)*

Frits Zernike, Dutch scientist awarded the 1953 Nobel Prize for Physics for his invention of the phase-contrast microscope. *(1888)*

Sports and Games

Duncan Keith, named one of the 100 Greatest National Hockey League Players; three-time Stanley Cup champion and two-time Olympic gold medalist. *(1983)*

Carli Lloyd, two-time Olympic gold medalist in soccer; twice named FIFA Player of the Year. *(1982)*

Adam Scott, Australian golfer ranked World No. 1 in 2014; first Australian to win the Masters Tournament. *(1980)*

Kim Rhode, American double trap and skeet shooter who won six Olympic medals in six consecutive games, including three gold medals; most successful female shooter in Olympic history. *(1979)*

Barry Sanders, running back for Oklahoma State and the Detroit Lions, two-time NFL Offensive Player of the Year, member of the College Football Hall of Fame and the Pro Football Hall of Fame. *(1968)*

Phil Hellmuth, professional poker player who set a record of fourteen World Series of Poker bracelets; member of the Poker Hall of Fame. *(1964)*

Dennis Priestley, won two world championships in darts. *(1950)*

Ron Yary, offensive tackle for USC, the Minnesota Vikings, and the Los Angeles Rams; member of the College Football Hall of Fame and the Pro Football Hall of Fame. *(1946)*

James Johnson, led the Dallas Cowboys to two Super Bowl wins as head coach, and served as head coach at Oklahoma State University-Stillwater and the University of Miami; member of the College Football Hall of Fame. *(1943)*

Margaret Court, tennis player who amassed more major titles than any other player in history, ranked World No. 1 in 1962; member of the International Tennis Hall of Fame. *(1942)*

Max McGee, wide receiver for the Green Bay Packers, best remembered for his seven receptions for 138 yards and two touchdowns in the first Super Bowl; later a major partner in developing the Chi-Chi's chain of Mexican restaurants. *(1932)*

Shoeless Joe Jackson, baseball outfielder primarily for the Chicago White Sox; accused of being part of the Black Sox Scandal, a conspiracy to fix the World Series, although there is controversy about his guilt. The saying "Say it ain't so, Joe," refers to him. *(1887)* *(Photo page 18.)*

Writing

Tony Kushner, playwright and screenwriter who won the 1993 Pulitzer Prize for Drama for *Angels in America*; nominated for Academy Awards for the 2005's *Munich* and 2012's *Lincoln*. (1956)

Margaret Court in 1970 (Photo: Spaarnestad Photo/Nationaal Archief, CC BY-SA 3.0)

Sheri S. Tepper, science fiction, horror, and mystery novelist who received the 2015 World Fantasy Award for Life Achivement. *(1929)*

Robert Sheckley, science fiction writer best known for the 1953 short story "Seventh Victim," adapted into the 1965 film *The 10th Victim,* starring Marcello Mastroianni and Ursula Andress; author of numerous absurdist and comedic works *(1928)*

Shirley Hughes, author and illustrator of more than 50 books; received two Kate Greenaway Medals for British children's books as well as the Booktrust lifetime achievement award. Her best known work in 1977's *Dogger.* *(1927)*

Kathleen Norris, author of 93 novels, many of them best sellers; one of the most popular American novelists of the first half of the 20th century. *(1880)*

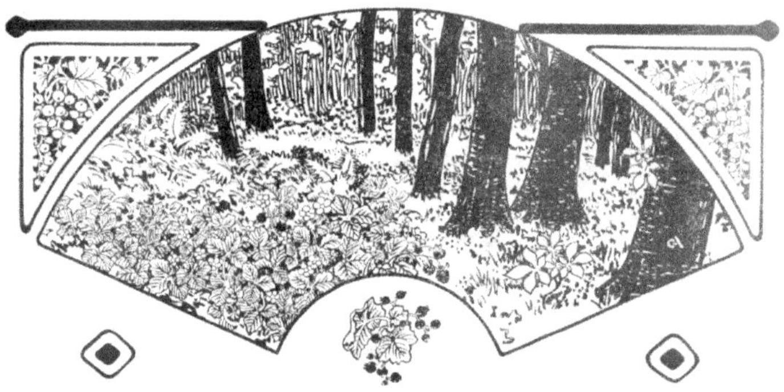

July, by George Auriol

Poster for *The 10th Victim*, based on a story by **Robert Sheckley**

Time magazine cover by Boris Artzybasheff

Who Died on July 16?

Art and Illustration

Morris, Belgian cartoonist best known as the creator of *Lucky Luke. (2001)*

Robert Motherwell, artist and printmaker of the New York School of abstract expressionist and surrealist painting. *(1991)*

Boris Artzybasheff (Борис Арцыбашев), illustrator known for his surreal designs; painted over 200 covers for *Time* magazine. *(1965)*

Giuseppe Crespi, Italian painter of the late Baroque period, considered one of the Old Masters. *(1747)*

Business

Masaharu Matsushita (松下 正治), second president of Panasonic and son-in-law of its founder; credited with turning Panasonic into a global brand. *(2012)*

Government and Politics

John F. Kennedy, Jr., son of US President John F. Kennedy; died in a plane crash with his wife and sister-in-law. *(1999)*

Frank Rizzo, controversial Philadelphia police commissioner and mayor involved in racial strife and scandals during his tenure. *(1991)*

Mary Todd Lincoln, First Lady of the United States during the administration of her husband Abraham Lincoln. *(1882)*

Mary Todd Lincoln (Photo: Mathew Brady/Levin C. Handy)

Anne of Cleves, Queen of England and fourth wife of Henry VIII. *(1557)*

Anne of Cleves, by Hans Holbein the Younger

Military

Charles Sweeney, US Army Air Force pilot of the B-29 *Bockscar,* which dropped the atomic bomb on the Japanese city of Nagasaki. *(2004)*

Albert Kesselring, German field marshal and Luftwaffe commander during World War II; convicted of war crimes at Nuremberg. *(1960)*

Music

Johnny Winter, singer-songwriter and multi-instrumentalist named to the Blues Foundation Hall of Fame. *(2014)*

Kitty Wells, country music singer who became the first female to reach #1 on the country charts with her 1952 hit "It Wasn't God Who Made Honky Tonk Angels." Received a Grammy Lifetime Achievement Award and was inducted into the Country Music Hall of Fame. *(2012)* *(Photo page 42.)*

Jo Stafford, pop singer known for her 1952 hit "You Belong to Me." *(2008)*

Celia Cruz, Cuban singer who became the most popular Latin artist of the 20th century, with 23 gold albums; received the US National Medal of Arts. *(2003)*

Johnny Winter (Photo: John Kadvany, CC BY-SA 3.0)

 Michael Dobson

Kitty Wells

Harry Chapin (Photo: Cindy Funk, CC BY-SA 2.0)

Herbert von Karajan, principal conductor of the Berlin Philharmonic for 35 years; considered to be one of the top-selling classical music recording artists of all time. *(1989)*

Harry Chapin, singer-songwriter known for his hits "Cat's in the Cradle," "W*O*L*D," and "Taxi." Received a Presidential Gold Medal for his role in the creation of the 1977 Presidential Commission on World Hunger. *(1981)*

Performing Arts

George A. Romero, filmmaker known for his zombie apocalypse and horror films, beginning with 1968's *Night of the Living Dead. (2017)*

William Asher, creator and producer of television shows including *Our Miss Brooks* and *Bewitched,* which starred his then-wife Elizabeth Montgomery. *(2012)*

Religion

Ellen G. White, one of the founders of the Seventh-Day Adventist Church, named one of the 100 Most Significant American Figures by *Smithsonian* magazine. *(1915)*

Science

Julian Schwinger, shared the 1965 Nobel Prize in Physics for his work on quantum electrodynamics. *(1994)*

Sports

Buck Buchanan, defensive tackle for Grambling College and the Kansas City Chiefs; member of the College Football Hall of Fame and the Pro Football Hall of Fame. *(1992)*

Writing and Speaking

Stephen Covey, motivational author and speaker best known for his book *The 7 Habits of Highly Effective People.* (2012)

Carol Shields, received the Pulitzer Prize for Fiction for her 1993 novel *The Stone Diaries.* (2003)

Stephen Spender, English poet and novelist who received a knighthood and served as United States Poet Laureate. *(1995)*

Heinrich Böll, German author who received the 1972 Nobel Prize for Literature. *(1985)*

John P. Marquand, author of the *Mr. Moto* spy series; won the 1938 Pulitzer Prize for Fiction for *The Late George Apley.* (1960)

Hilaire Belloc, Anglo-French writer and historian considered one of the greatest names in Edwardian letters, frequent collaborator with G. K. Chesterton. *(1953)*

Ned Buntline, best known for his dime novels about the Old West; helped publicize famous Wild West personalities including Buffalo Bill Cody and Wild Bill Hickok. *(1886)*

From left to right: **Ned Buntline,** Buffalo Bill Cody, Giuseppina Morlacchi, and Texas Jack Omohundro, circa 1873.

Anne Askew, one of the earliest known female poets to write in the English language; first Englishwoman to demand a divorce; condemned as a heretic during the reign of Henry VIII and became the only woman to be tortured in the Tower of London and burnt at the stake. *(1546)*

Quote of the Day

"I have wandered all my life, and I have also traveled; the difference between the two being this, that we wander for distraction, but we travel for fulfillment."

Hilaire Belloc, writer and poet
died July 16, 1953

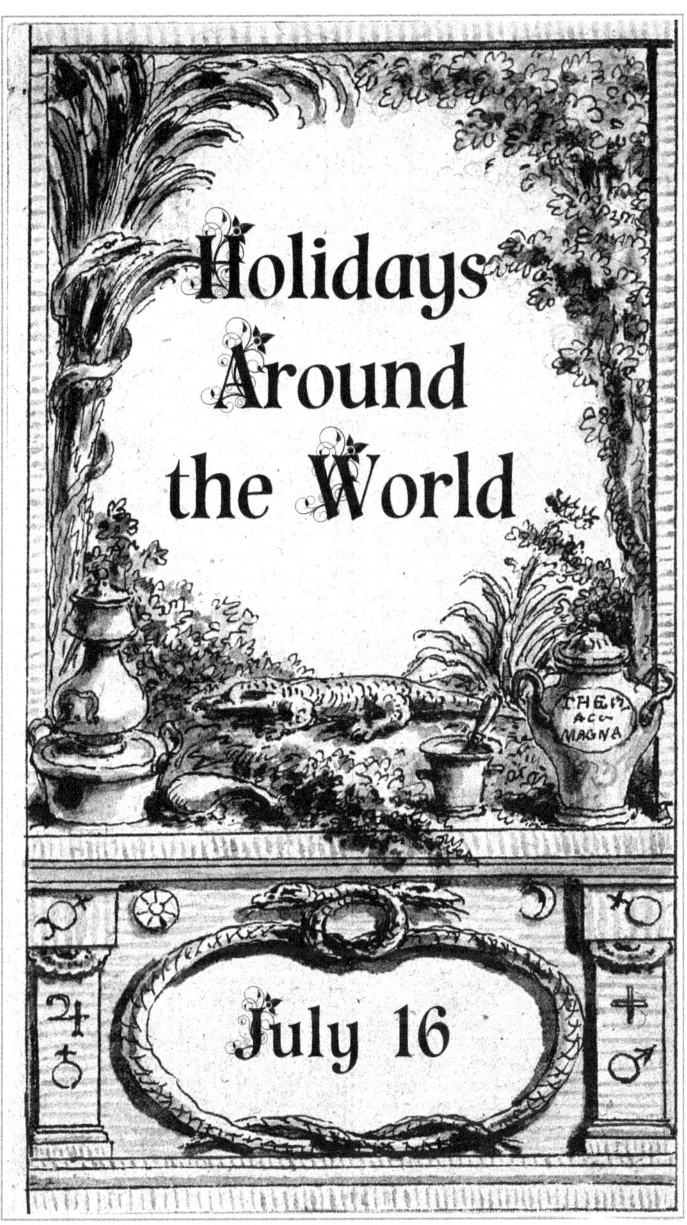

Holidays
Around
the World

THEM
ACC
MAGNA

July 16

Promotional poster for snake charmer Nala Damajanti at the
Folies Bergère, 1886 — for **World Snake Day**

July 16 Holidays and Celebrations

If you're looking for a reason to take your special day off, you should know that every single day is a holiday somewhere in the world! Here's some of what you can celebrate on July 16!

General Events

Día del Ingeniero Civil (Honduras)
The nation of Honduras honors its civil engineers on July 16 each year.

Holocaust Memorial Day (France)
France has an annual day of commemoration honoring victims, survivors, and rescuers of the Holocaust. The date of July 16 marks the anniversary of the 1942 Vel' d'Hiv Roundup, in which more than 13,000 Paris Jews were arrested and sent to Auschwitz.

World Snake Day (international)
There are nearly 3,500 known species of snakes worldwide, most of which are fairly harmless and some of which are endangered. The Advocates for Snake Preservation created World Snake Day on July 16 to celebrate snakes and raise awareness about their conservation.

"Our Lady of Mount Carmel," from the workshop of Manoel da Costa Ataíde — for the **Feast of Our Lady of Carmel**

Religious Feast Days and Holidays

Saint Days

Each day in the year is considered a feast day for one or more saints. They are somewhat different in western Christianity (Catholicism and many forms of Protestantism) and in eastern (Orthodox) Christianity. There are many others; this is a selection.

In *Western Christianity*, July 16 is the feast day of Saints Gondulphus of Tongeren, Helier, and Reineldis, and also the feast day of Our Lady of Mount Carmel, the title of the Virgin Mary as patroness of the Carmelite Order.

In *Eastern Orthodox Christianity*, it is also the commemoration of the Hieromartyr Athenogenes and his disciples, and Martyrs Antiochus of Sebaste, Faustus, and Julia of Carthage. (These saints are honored on July 29 by "Old Calendrists.‡")

---

‡ "Old Calendrists" use the older Julian calendar rather than the modern Gregorian calendar for liturgical purposes. For more about the different types of calendars, see "What Day of the Week is July 16?"

Moveable and Multi-Day Events

Some events take place over a specific week or time period. Start and finish dates may vary from year to year. Some events occur on different days each year (such as "fourth Saturday of a month"). These events sometimes take place on or include July 16.

Beginning of the Hindu month of Mithuna (mid-June)

- *Raja Parba* (ରଜ ପର୍ବ), three-day festival to mark the beginning of the agricultural year in the Indian state of Odisha *(Varies between March and July)*
- *Phi Ta Khon*, also known as the Ghost Festival, is a three-day Buddhist celebration in Loei province, Thailand. The date is selected annually by each town's spirit mediums.

Week Including June 12

- National Automotive Service Professionals Week (US)

Monday after the Second Saturday

- Queen's Official Birthday (Norfolk Island)

An automobile mechanic at work, by Arne F. Køpke (National Archives of Norway, CC BY-SA 4.0) — for **National Automotive Service Professionals Week**

Celebrations About Food

In the United States, almost every day of the year is dedicated to a particular food — some days honor more than one!. Sponsored by manufacturers, retailers, farmers, or simply fans, these days are often proclaimed by the President, Congress, state governors, or mayors.

In the US, July 16 is both **National Ice Cream Day** and **National Corn Fritter Day**, though we don't recommend combining the two.

If July 16 falls on the third Saturday of the month, it's also Strawberry Rhubarb Wine Day.

The entire month of July is dedicated to the following foods.

- National Baked Beans Month
- National Blueberry Month
- National Candy Month
- National Culinary Arts Month
- National Fruit and Veggies Month
- National Grilling Month
- National Honey Month
- National Hot Dog Month
- National Ice Cream Month
- National Pickle Month
- National Picnic Month
- National Rosé Wine Month
- National Watermelon Month

People eating hot dogs, from the 1914 film *Josie's Coney Island Nightmare* — for **National Hot Dog Month**

The New York Marble Bar and Ice Cream Parlor, 1912 — for **National Ice Cream Day and Month**

A young girl talking with her Marine Corps father returning from Iraq (Credit: Sgt. Randall A. Clinton, USMC) — for **National Black Family Month** and **Cell Phone Courtesy Month**

Honorary Months

Presidents, Congresses, and nations around the world issue proclamations recognizing particular months to honor certain causes. These events generally fall in July, though honorary months do come and go.

Health

- Bereaved Parents Awareness Month
- Fragile X Awareness Month
- Group B Strep Awareness Month (US, UK)
- Herbal/Prescription Interaction Awareness Month
- Juvenile Arthritis Awareness Month
- National Wheelchair Beautification Month

Recreation

- Family Golf Month
- National Park and Recreation Month
- National Vacation Rental Month
- Women's Motorcycle Month

Society

- Cell Phone Courtesy Month
- Get Ready for Kindergarten Month
- National Black Family Month

Moveable Events

Some celebrations shift their dates from year to year, occurring on the "first Thursday" or "fourth weekend." Here are some moveable events that sometimes include July 16.

- Celebration of the Horse Day *(third weekend)*
- Lake Superior Day *(third Sunday)*

Just for Fun

Anybody can make up a holiday, and many people do! While none of these are officially recognized and some may come and go, here are a few more holidays for July 16.

- Family History Day
- International Bath Day (celebrates Archimedes' famous bathtub discovery)
- International Surfing Day *(third Saturday)*
- National Flip Flop Day *(third Friday)*, United States

A 1911 surfer girl, by J. A. Cahill— for **International Surfing Day**

Quote of the Day

"The English winter — ending in July,
To recommence in August."

— Lord Byron, *Don Juan*"

About
the
Month
of
July

July, from the *Brevarium Grimani* by Gerard Horenbout and Simon Bening (c.1510)

July: The Seventh Month

> *"Hot July brings cooling showers,*
> *Apricots and gillyflowers."*
> — *Sara Coleridge, "The Months".*

In the original Roman calendar, the month of July was named *Quintilis*, the fifth month, because the Romans originally counted the first of March as the beginning of the new year.

Quintilis was renamed July by the Roman senate in honor of Gaius Julius Caesar after his death in 44 BCE, because Caesar, among his other accomplishments, had undertaken a major calendar reform, known as the Julian calendar, which remained the standard European calendar until 1582 CE. (Not to be outdone, Emperor Augustus arranged for the next month, Sextilis, to be renamed in his honor.)

July is one of the seven months with 31 days. In a common (non-leap) year, it always starts on the same day of the week as April, and on the same day of the week as January in leap years. Strangely, in common years, no other month of the year ends on the same day of the week as July! (In leap years, the last day of July and January fall on the same day.)

July in Other Cultures

In Latin, the month of July was spelled *Iulius*, as the Romans did not have the letter "J."

In Albanian, the month is *korrik*. Arabs call the month يوليه *(yūlia)*.

It is юли *(juli)* in Bulgaria, *lipanj* in Croatia, and *červen* in Czech.

The Finns call the month *kesäkuu* and the Greeks call it Ιούλιος *(Ioúlios)*.

The Hebrew calendar has different months, but when they refer to the Gregorian month, it's יולי *(yûlî)*.

In Gaelic, July is *Meitheamh mi an Mheitheamh,* and in Russian, it is июнь *(ijun')*.

The Chinese use 六月 *(liùyuè* in Mandarin); Koreans 유월 *(yuweol);* and it's 腸趷 *(tháng sáu)* in Vietnamese.

July Sayings and Superstitions

Farming

- The corn harvest will be good if the corn growing in the fields is "knee high by the Fourth of July."
- "If the first of July be rainy weather, 'twill rain more or less for four weeks together."
- "Rain or dry, plant your turnips on the Fourth of July."

- A swarm of bees in May is worth a load of hay. A swarm of bees in June is worth a silver spoon. A swarm of bees in July is not worth a fly.

Marriage

- "Those who in July do wed, must labor for their daily bread."

As for which day of the week, that's easy.

Monday for health, Tuesday for wealth,
Wednesday best of all, Thursday for losses,
Friday for crosses, Saturday for no luck at all.

July Symbols

Birthstone: Ruby (symbolizes success, devotion, and integrity.)

According to an old English proverb, "The glowing Ruby should adorn/Those who in warm July are born,/Then will they be exempt and free/From love's doubt and anxiety."

Ruby

Birth Flowers: Water Lily (purity of heart) or Larkspur (lightness and levity.)

Water Lily (Photo: Dinkum)

Birth Tree: Elm (strength of will and intuition)

"Study of an Elm Tree," John Constable (1821)

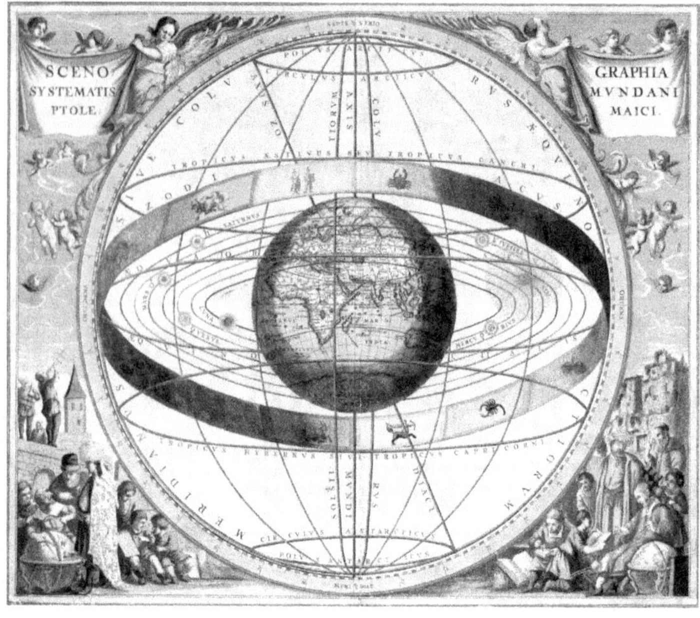

Scenography of the Ptolemaic Cosmography, by Johannes van Loon, based on Andreas Cellarius's *Harmonia Macrocosmica,* 1660

July 16 Zodiac Signs

From the perspective of someone on Earth, the Sun appears to move through the sky throughout the year, along a path astronomers call the *ecliptic plane*. The ecliptic plane is divided into twelve constellations, known as the zodiac, based on traditionally observed patterns of stars. On your birthday, you can't see your constellation, because it's in the daytime sky.

The zodiac was first developed by Babylonian astronomers about 2,500 years ago. Because they were unaware that the Earth wobbles like a spinning top (known as *precession*), they didn't make allowance for the fact that the Sun's path through the zodiac changes over time.

That means there are now two sets of dates for your birth sign. The *tropical dates* are the original Babylonian dates; the *sidereal dates* tell you where the Sun actually appears as it moves along its annual path.

July 16, however, is one of the few days each year in which the tropical and sidereal sign is the same: **Cancer.**

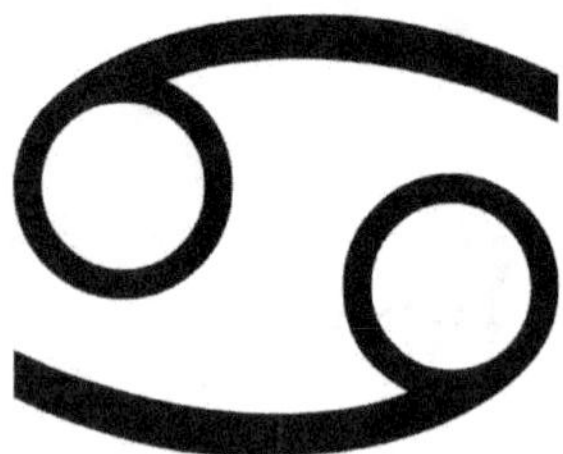

Cancer

Tropical June 21 to July 22
Sidereal July 16 to August 15

The Greek word for "crab" is Καρκινος (Karkinos), later Latinized as carcinus, which evolved into our word cancer. In Greek mythology. In one telling, when Hercules was battling the Hydra, Zeus's wife Hera sent Karkinos to distract the hero, but Hercules kicked it with such force that it was thrown into the sky, becoming a constellation. (Some say that Hercules crushed the crab with his foot and that Hera placed the crab in the night sky as a reward for its service.)

Because of the association with the disease, some astrologers refer to those born under the sign of Cancer as "moon children," because the ruling planet of Cancer is the Moon.

Cancers (or Moon Children) are supposed to be loyal, dependable, caring, and adaptable, but can also be moody, self-pitying, and oversensitive. Cancers are supposed to be particularly compatible with Scorpios, Piceans, and other Cancers.

The Sign of Cancer, by Giovanni Maria Falconetto (Courtesy Palazzo d'Arco, Mantua, Italy)

Illustration by Edward Penfield

What Day of the Week is July 16?

On what day of the week does July 16 fall?

Surprisingly, this isn't an easy question. Because the calendar year is 365 days long (366 in leap years), it doesn't divide evenly by the seven days of the week.

Also, the Earth goes around the Sun in about 365-1/4 days, so a calendar tends to drift over time. That's why the same date falls on different weekdays in different years.

This is made even more complicated by a change in calendars that took place in 1582. Our modern calendar has its roots in ancient Rome, in a calendar reform conducted by Julius Caesar. Caesar commissioned mathematicians to attack the problem, and they came up with the idea of leap years, and thus standardized the calendar for centuries to come. This was called the Julian calendar.

Over time, however, the small errors in Caesar's calculation compounded. That's why Pope Gregory XIII commissioned the Gregorian calendar, used in most of the world today. Some countries converted in 1582, when the calendar was first developed; some converted later; other still haven't changed.

Gregorian and Julian aren't the only types of calendars. The Hebrew year, the Islamic year, and many other calendars are used in different parts of the world and among different people.

You can convert Gregorian dates to other calendars, including the Hebrew calendar, the Islamic calendar, and even the Mayan calendar by visiting the Fourmilab Calendar Converter at http://www.fourmilab.ch/documents/calendar/.

Chinese calendar systems are quite complex and have changed several times; a full discussion is far beyond the scope of this book. If you're interested, you can find information here: http://www.hermetic.ch/cal_stud/chinese_cal.htm.

On Names and Dates

Historians use "CE" (Common Era) and "BCE" (Before the Common Era) instead of the more common "AD" (Anno Domini, or Year of Our Lord) and "BC" (Before Christ), reflecting the fact that the year-numbering system established by the Gregorian calendar is used throughout the world in many countries not culturally Christian.

The CE/BCE designation dates back to at least 1708, and has been adopted as a standard by the United Nations and the Universal Postal Union. Because this series of books covers events and people of all nations and cultures, we use the CE/BCE terms.

The abbreviation "O.S." ("Old Style") and "N.S." ("New Style") on some dates refers to the fact that the Russian Empire (in particular) did not switch from the Julian to the Gregorian calendar at the same time as the rest of Europe, and therefore some figures and events have two dates.

Also, in the Julian calendar in England in the 16th century, the year began on March 25 rather than January 1. To avoid confusion with Gregorian dates, dates between January and March were often written using both years.

People and events whose original names are not in the Western alphabet have their native names (where possible) in the appropriate script shown in parenthesis. If you are using an e-reader to access an electronic version of this book, all characters don't always display on all devices.

A 50-year brass perpetual calendar.

Quote of the Day

"Time is an illusion, lunchtime doubly so."

Douglas Adams,
from *The Hitchhiker's Guide to the Galaxy*

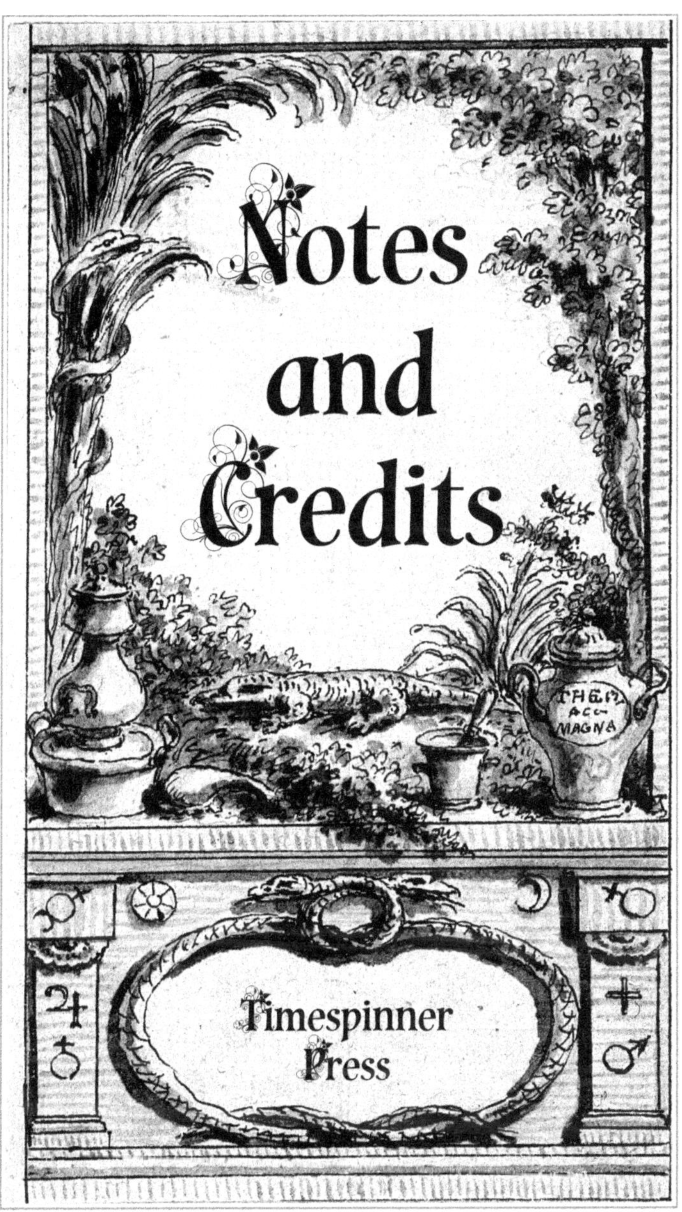
Notes
and
Credits
THER
ACC
MAGNA
Timespinner
Press

Cartoon by John T. McCutcheon

Copyright, Credit, and Contact

Follow Us

Our blog "This Day in History" (http://
timespinnerpress.com/this-day-in-history/) features short
articles on events and people associated with each day, and
updates several times each week. Also subscribe to the
"Quote of the Day" at http://timespinnerpress.com/quote-
of-the-day/. You can get daily links by following us on
Facebook at TimespinnerPress, or on Twitter as
@sidewisethinker.

Contact Us

Find an error or a format problem? Want information about
the series, about us, or about when the volume for your
special day might be available? Please email us at
editor@timespinnerpress.com. (We also take requests if your
special day isn't yet complete. Please give us at least six
weeks' notice if possible.)

Sources

We owe a great debt to Wikipedia, which is our first stop for
research. We attempt to make independent confirmation of
all important dates and facts through a variety of other
sources.

Other sources we frequently use include the Library of
Congress; "on this day" listings from *Encyclopedia Britannica*,
the *New York Times*, and the BBC; Omniglot for the names of
months in other languages; *Chase's Calendar of Events;* and, of
course, the always essential Google.

All art and photographs are either in the public domain, used under a Creative Commons license, or with a "fair use" justification, and most frequently come from Wikimedia Commons and the Library of Congress Prints and Photographs Division.

Attribution is provided where possible, or as requested by the copyright owner, or when there is particular historical significance, listed below. For information about any particular illustration or photograph, please contact us.

Credits

1. The cover photograph of Apollo 11 in flight with the American flag in the foreground was taken July 16, 1969. It is in the public domain as a work solely created by NASA, and carries the photo ID GPN-2000-000627 and alternate ID 69PC-0397.

2. The illustration of the month of July used on the back cover is from the French Gothic illuminated manuscript *Les Très Riches Heures du duc de Berry* by the Limbourg Brothers, Jean Colombe, and an intermediate painter whose name is lost to history. It is in the public domain because its copyright has expired.

3. The box graphic used on the first page is from a 1916 pamphlet entitled "Divorce versus Democracy" authored by G. K. Chesterton, originally published in London by the Society of St. Peter and St. Paul. It is in the public domain in the US because it was published prior to 1923, and is in the public domain in all countries (including the country of origin) in which the copyright time is the author's life plus 70 years or less.

4. The graphic design for the section pages in this book is from a design originally created for a pharmacy label. It is courtesy of Wellcome Images (ICV No 11073, photo V0010813), and is used here under CC BY-SA 4.0.

5. The 1846 illustration *July* by Eugène Grasset w is in the public domain because its copyright has expired.

6. The photograph of the liftoff of Apollo 11 is in the public domain as a work created solely by NASA.

7. The photograph of the crew of Apollo 11 is in the public domain as a work created solely by NASA.

8. The photograph of the Apollo 11 lunar module is in the public domain as a work created solely by NASA.

9. The photograph of the first step on the Moon is in the public domain as a work created solely by NASA.

10. The photograph of the plaque of Apollo 11 is in the public domain as a work created solely by NASA.

11. The photograph of Buzz Aldrin on the Moon is in the public domain as a work created solely by NASA.

12. The 17th century banknote from Stockholms Banco is in the public domain because its copyright has expired.

13. The 1889 chromolithograph of the First Battle of Bull Run by Kurz & Allison is in the public domain because its copyright has expired.

14. The painting of the Mission San Diego de Alcalá in 1848 originally appeared in the 1920 book *Mission San Diego*, by Zephyrin Engelhardt. It is in the public domain because it was first published in the US prior to January 1, 1923.

15. The 1913 photograph of Shoeless Joe Jackson by Charles M. Conlon is in the public domain because its copyright has expired. The image has been cropped.

16. The 1937 publicity photo of Ginger Rogers is in the public domain because it was first published in the United States between 1923 and 1977 without a copyright notice. Typically, publicity photographs are not copyrighted because of the way in which they are intended to be used.

17. The 1979 publicity photo of Orville Redenbacher is in the public domain because it was first published in the United States between 1978 and 1989 without a copyright notice, and its copyright was not subsequently registered with the US Copyright Office within five years of publication.

18. The 1893 photograph of Ida B. Wells-Barnett by Mary Garrity is in the public domain because its copyright has expired. It is from the collection of the US National Portrait Gallery, NPG.2009.36.

19. The 1899 photograph of Roald Amundsen by Daniel Georg Nyblin is in the public domain because its copyright has expired. It is from the collection of the National Library of Norway.

20. The 2009 photograph of Michael Flatley is by Max Lin, and is used here under CC BY-SA 2.0. The image has been cropped.

21. The 1957 photograph of Bess Myerson is in the public domain because it was first published in the United States between 1923 and 1977 without a copyright notice.

22. The 1920 photograph of Larry Semon is in the public domain because its copyright has expired.

23. The 1937 photograph of Barbara Stanwyck in *Stella Dallas* is in the public domain because it was first published in the United States between 1923 and 1977 without a copyright notice.

24. The 1942 screenshot from the film *George Washington Slept Here* is in the public domain because it was first published in the United States between 1923 and 1977 without a copyright notice. Traditionally, motion picture trailers were not copyrighted because of the way in which they were intended to be used, even though the films themselves were copyrighted.

25. The 1970 photograph of Margaret Court is from the Dutch National Archives and Spaarnestad Photo, used here under the CC BY-SA 3.0 Netherlands license.

26. The 1912 illustration of the month of July by George Auriol is in the public domain because its copyright has expired.

27. The Italian movie poster for the film *La Decima Vittima* may or may not carry a copyright notice. Typically, movie posters are not copyrighted because of the way in which they are intended to be used. If it is copyrighted, its use here is under "fair use" provisions of the copyright code. It illustrates a person and event of historic interest, no free equivalent is available, the image is of a size and resolution not suitable for counterfeit work, and its use here does not impair the copyright owner's ability to market it elsewhere.

28. The cover of the January 6, 1958, issue of *Time* magazine is in the public domain because it was published in the United

States between 1923 and 1963, and although it was originally copyrighted, the copyright was not renewed.

29. The photograph of Mary Todd Lincoln was taken by photographers Mathew Brady and Levin C. Handy between 1860 and 1865, and is in the public domain because its copyright has expired. It is from the Brady-Handy Collection at the Library of Congress (digital ID cwpbh.03451)

30. The portrait of Anne of Cleves by Hans Holbein the Younger was painted circa 1539 and is n the public domain because its copyright has expired. It can be seen the the Louvre Museum, Paris.

31. The 1969 photograph of Johnny Winter is by John Kadvany, and is used here under CC BY-SA 3.0.

32. The 1957 photograph of Kitty Wells is from the *Grand Ole Opry Souvenir Picture Album*. It is in the public domain because it was published in the United States between 1923 and 1963, and although it may or may not have carried a copyright notice, the copyright was not renewed.

33. The photograph of Harry Chapin is by Cindy Funk, and is used here under CC BY-SA 2.0.

34. The 1873 photograph of Buffalo Bill Cody and others is in the public domain because its copyright has expired.

35. The 1886 promotional poster for Nala Damajanti at the Folies Bergère was printed by F. Appel. It is in the public domain because its copyright has expired.

36. The 18th century painting of Our Lady of Mount Carmel is from the workshop of Manoel da Costa Ataíde, and is in the public domain because its copyright has expired.

37. The 1952 photograph of an automobile mechanic at work was taken by Arne F. Køpke, and is from the collection of the National Archives of Norway (RA/PA-0797/U/Ua/L0016/0273). It is used here under CC BY-SA 4.0 International.

38. The 1914 photograph from the film *Josie's Coney Island Nightmare* is from the Billy Rose Theatre Collection, New York Public Library, digital ID TH-2471. It is in the public domain because its copyright has expired.

39. The 1912 photograph of the New York Marble Bar and Ice Cream Parlor, Brisbane, Australia, is from the collection of

the State Library of Queensland (accession number 6841). It is in the public domain because its copyright has expired.

40. The 2009 photograph of a girl talking with her father was taken by Sgt. Randall A. Clinton, USMC, and was released by the Marine Corps with the ID 091125-M-4003C-034. It is in the public domain as a work created by an employee of the US government as part of that person's official duties.

41. The July 1911 cover of *Sunset* magazine, illustrated by J. A. Cahill, is in the public domain because its first publication occurred prior to January 1, 1923.

42. The painting "July" is from the *Brevarium Grimani*, by Gerard Horenbout and Simon Bening, and was created circa 1510. It is in the public domain because its copyright has expired.

43. The photograph of a ruby was released into the public domain by its creator.

44. The photograph of a water lily at Kew Gardens was taken by "Dinkum," who released it into the public domain under the CC0 1.0 dedication.

45. The 1821 painting "Study of an Elm Tree" by John Constable is in the public domain because its copyright has expired. The painting is in the collection of the Victoria & Albert Museum, London.

46. The celestial sphere is from *Scenography of the Ptolemaic Cosmography*, by Johannes van Loon, based on Andreas Cellarius's *Harmonia Macrocosmica*, 1660. It is in the public domain because its copyright has expired.

47. The fresco "Sign of Cancer" by Giovanni Maria Falconetto was painted between 1515 and 1520, and is in the public domain because its copyright has expired. The image is courtesy Palazzo d'Arco, Mantua, Italy.

48. The 1906 automobile calendar is by Edward Penfield, and is in the collection of the Library of Congress Prints and Photographs Division. It is in the public domain because its copyright has expired.

49. The 50-year perpetual calendar photograph is in the public domain.

50. The cartoon by John T. McCutcheon is from his 1905 collection *The Mysterious Stranger and Other Cartoons* by John T. McCutcheon. It is in the public domain because its copyright has expired.

51. The painting of July from *Labors of the Month* by Simon Bening was created in the first half of the 16th century, and is in the public domain because its copyright has expired.
52. The painting *July* by Joachim von Sandrart was created in 1642, and is in the public domain because its copyright has expired. It is in the collection of the Staatsgalerie im Neuen Schloss, Schleißheim, Germany.

License Description and Terms

Aside from material purely in the public domain, photographs and other material in this book are used under specific licenses permitting free use, usually with an attribution requirement. For full text and terms of these licenses, click or enter the appropriate links below. If you believe there is an error in the copyright status or attribution of any of these images, please email us.

- Creative Commons Attribution 2.0 Generic (CC-BY 2.0): http://creativecommons.org/licenses/by/2.0/deed.en
- Creative Commons Attribution-Share Alike 3.0 Generic (CC-BY-SA 3.0): http://creativecommons.org/licenses/by-sa/3.0/
- Creative Commons Attribution-Share Alike 2.5 Generic (CC-BY-SA 2.5): http://creativecommons.org/licenses/by-sa/2.5/deed.en
- Creative Commons Attribution-Share Alike 2.0 Generic (CC-BY-SA 2.0): http://creativecommons.org/licenses/by/2.0/deed.en
- Creative Commons Attribution-Share Alike 1.0 Generic (CC-BY-SA 1.0): http://creativecommons.org/licenses/by-sa/1.0/deed.en
- CC0 1.0 Universal (CC0 1.0) Public Domain Dedication (CC0 1.0) http://creativecommons.org/publicdomain/zero/1.0/deed.en
- GNU Free Documentation License (GFDL): http://en.wikipedia.org/wiki/Wikipedia:Text_of_the_GNU_Free_Documentation_License
- License Art Libre (Free Art License): http://artlibre.org

 Michael Dobson

July, from the *Brevarium Grimani* by Simon Bening (c.1510)

Other Books from Timespinner Press

The Story of a Special Day
Michael Dobson

A series of (eventually) 366 volumes covering everything that happened on your special day! Events, births, deaths, quotes, holidays, and much more. It's like a birthday card they'll never throw away!

US$7.95 print / US$2.99 ebook.

From Plassey to Pakistan
Humayun Mirza

The history of British Colonial India and the formation of Pakistan from the unique perspective of the son of Pakistan's first president and last of the royal line of Bengal, Bihar, and Orissa! This unique historical document tells the inside story of this distinguished family, including the detailed story of the coup that toppled his father from power!

US$27.95 print

A Whole New Navy: America's War in the Pacific

Miles Durr

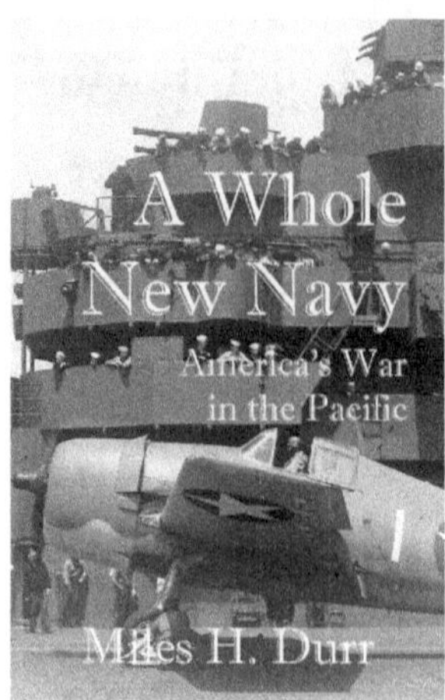

The most comprehensive and detailed description of America's naval war in the Pacific ever—every battle, every ship, every task force and every task group from Pearl Harbor through the Japanese surrender! A must-have for the collection of every World War II buff!

US$29.95 print

Improbable History: The Weird, the Obscure, and the Strangely Important

edited by Michael Dobson

From the birth of Western civilization to the rescue of Apollo 13, from the Leaning Tower of Pisa to Florence's Duomo, history has often turned on small, improbable details. Whatever happened to the ancient Samaritan people? Why did a fortuitous rainstorm allow the British to conquer India? How did an air raid in Italy lead to the development of chemotherapy? What happened when Albert Einstein met Adolf Hitler on the streets of Berlin? How did the Japanese manage to attack the US mainland using balloons? A cast of award-winning writers tackle some of the strangest tales in history!

US$19.95 print

July, by Joachim von Sandrart